THE SEARCH ~FOR~ RICHES

Andrew Langley

RSVP
RAINTREE
STECK-VAUGHN
P U B L I S H E R S
The Steck-Vaughn Company

Austin, Texas

THE REMARKABLE WORLD

Published by Raintree Steck-Vaughn Publishers, an imprint of Steck-Vaughn Company

Library of Congress Cataloging-in-Publication Data
Langley, Andrew.
The search for riches / Andrew Langley.
    p.   cm.—(Remarkable world)
Includes bibliographical references and index.
Summary: Describes how people throughout the world have looked for such valuable commodities as gold, jewels, oil, and buried treasure.
ISBN 0-8172-4544-8
1. Treasure-trove—Juvenile literature.
[1. Gold. 2. Precious stones. 3. Petroleum.
4. Buried treasure.]
I. Title. II. Series.
G525.L3535   1997
910.4'5—dc20   96-30797

Printed in Italy. Bound in the United States.
1 2 3 4 5 6 7 8 9 0 01 00 99 98 97

Picture acknowledgments
AKG London 39b; Bryan and Cherry Alexander 26, 29; Anglo-American Corporation Title page; Bridgeman Art Library 17t; Camera Press 16b/August Sycholt, 18b/August Sycholt, 38t/James Pickerell; Bruce Coleman Ltd. 28/Mr. Johnny Johnson; John Cruise-Wilkins 37 both; Sue Cunningham Photographic 32b, 33; De Beers 19 all; ET Archive 9, 22t, 41b; Fotomas Index 25t, 34t, 45; Hulton Deutsch 34–35, 35t, 40, 41t, 43b; Image Select 6t, 14b, 21; Mary Evans Picture Library 4b/Arthur Rackham Collection, 7b, 20b 43t; John Massey Stewart 25b; Peter Newark's Pictures 5b, 8t, 10t, 11 both, 12b, 13, 14t, 20t, 36, 44t; Photri 31t; Range/Bettmann 8b, 15b/RALL; Robert Harding 17b; Tony Stone Images *front cover* right, 4t/Penny Tweedie, 5t/Hans Peter Merten 27; Topham Picturepoint 16t; Trip 10b/W. Jacobs 23, 24 both; Wayland 22b; Zefa *front cover* center left and bottom left, 30 both, 44b. The artwork is by Barbara Loftus.

CONTENTS

WHY GOLD IS PRECIOUS

A modern jeweler in Kuwait City shows one of his gold necklaces to a female customer.

SOLDIERS have fought for gold. Explorers have braved uncharted oceans for it. Kings have been buried with it. Pirates have killed for it. What makes gold so alluring? Gold is beautiful, rare, and valuable. The gleam of pure gold never fades: It doesn't rust or tarnish like other metals. Gold coins left on the seabed for hundreds of years are still as bright as the day they were made. Gold is a perfect metal for making into jewelery and ornaments. It can be beaten easily into various shapes, or melted and cast in a mold. Every great civilization since the ancient Egyptians has made beautiful artifacts from gold. Even now, gold's value is powerful—and has changed the course of history many times.

King Midas touches flowers and turns them into gold in this illustration.

The Midas touch

According to Greek legend, there was once a king named Midas. He was granted one wish by the Greek god, Dionysus. Midas wished that everything he touched would turn to gold. And that's just what happened!

Midas touched his furniture, his house, his weapons—and they all changed to gold. He was delighted. Then a meal was laid before the hungry king. But when he picked it up, the food and wine turned into gold as well. Midas couldn't eat or drink. He had to beg the god to undo his wish. Dionysus told him to bathe in the Pactolus River, which has contained gold dust ever since.

After it has been purified, gold is cast into bars. Each bar is polished and stamped with its weight and number.

The Forty-Niners

John Sutter didn't set out to find gold. He was too busy running his huge ranch in the Sacramento Valley of California. But on one stormy day in 1848, gold came to him. Sutter was building a sawmill on the nearby American River. His construction chief, James Marshall, found some small, yellowish nuggets of gold on the riverbed. "My eye was caught by something shining in the bottom of the ditch.... I reached my hand down and picked it up; it made my heart thump, for I was certain it was gold." Sutter realized that he was sitting on a fortune.

Below John Sutter was already bankrupt when this portrait was painted in 1866.

He had to make sure other people would not find out, so he ordered his ranch hands to keep quiet.

Even so, the sensational news leaked out. At the end of the year, President James Polk revealed that the stories about Sutter's find were true, and his words set off the biggest gold rush of all time. Throughout 1849, fortune hunters swarmed into the Sacramento Valley from all over the world. More than 80,000 of these forty-niners reached the American River that year.

John Sutter's sawmill, where his construction chief James Marshall found a tiny gold nugget in the stream in 1848.

Left California during the Gold Rush years. The red dots show where gold was discovered between 1849 and 1859.

The lucky ones simply picked up nuggets where they lay on the ground. But most had to dig, pan, and scrabble for the precious metal.

The prospectors thought of nothing but gold. They rarely washed or changed clothes. Each one had staked a claim of land, where they worked all day in the intense heat of the sun. At night, they slept on their claim to prevent rivals from moving in.

Gradually, the gold rush spread northward, into the foothills of the Sierra Mountains, and camps sprang up. They were rough, violent places with names like Dead Man's Hollow and Hell's Half-Acre. Around the camps, towns began to spring up where prospectors could take their gold to be weighed and valued. But there were saloons and dance halls where fortunes could be squandered, and thieves loitered, eager to pick up gold the easy way.

By 1859, the great California Gold Rush was over. It had made a few people very rich, but many had left in ruin and despair. Among them was poor John Sutter. His estate was destroyed by the flood of forty-niners, and he lost all his money and land. He died in 1880, almost penniless.

Prospectors head for the California goldfields. They are loaded down with supplies and tools, including shovels, picks, and gold pans.

Pans and Long Toms

Gold dust lay on the beds of rivers and streams, but it was mixed with mud, sand, and gravel. The simplest way to separate them was to use a metal dish called a pan. The forty-niners spent countless hours crouched by the running water, scooping up sand and sloshing it around. The light grains of sand spilled over the sides, but the heavier gold remained.

A prospector uses a scoop to pour water through mud in a Long Tom to find gold.

It was very slow work. To speed things up, some prospectors built a "Long Tom." This was a long, wooden trough used to wash gold-bearing earth. The water and sand seeped out through holes at the end, leaving the gold behind.

The man in the foreground is panning for gold, while his partner uses a Long Tom.

Down under

Meanwhile, in Australia, gold was discovered near Ballarat, Victoria, in 1851. Immediately, the state went crazy. Shopkeepers left their shops, clerks left their banks, teachers even left their schools. When ships put into Melbourne harbor, their crews deserted.

All these people raced off to the goldfields. They heard tales of amazing finds. Nuggets could be picked up from the ground and from sandy stream beds. Some of these stories were true. Better still, several monster nuggets were unearthed. One of them, the Holtermann Nugget, weighed 628 pounds and stood more than four feet high.

Melbourne became a boomtown. In 1852 alone, 94,664 people arrived there by ship—more than 1,800 new arrivals a week. The streets were full of drunken miners who had made it rich. Some lit cigars with bank notes, or paraded through the town in grand carriages.

But Melbourne was paradise compared to the goldfields themselves. The land all around Ballarat had been torn to pieces by the diggers. They lived in villages of tents or wooden huts. At night, these settlements rang with the noise of fighting.

The Holtermann Nugget was huge. Its size can be seen clearly from this old photograph showing the nugget next to a man. The word *nugget* originated in Australia.

9

Right A map of the Klondike Gold Rush and the notorious Skagway route that led to Klondike and Dawson City

The cry of "Gold!" brought hundreds of hopeful prospectors from all corners of America and Europe. They faced a terrible journey, over 700 miles of deep snow, raging rivers, thick pine forests, and wild winds.

First, they had to get past the rogues of Skagway. Most prospectors landed here to be greeted by teams of respectable-looking men, anxious to offer advice. The "helpers" had only one aim, however—to rob the unwary arrivals. Frank Thomas of Indiana wrote home from Skagway in 1897 describing life among the prospectors. "There are thousands of people here...all mad and crazy just like us.... I am undoubtedly a crazy fool for being here in this God-forsaken country, but I have the consolation of seeing thousands of other men in all stages of life, rich and poor, wise and foolish, here in the same plight as I."

Prospectors fight their way through the snow and forests around Skagway in 1898

CANADA

Dawson City
Klondike

Nome

ALASKA (USA)

Skagway

12

The next barrier was the massive Chilkoot Pass. Up this steep, icy slope trudged an endless line of people and pack animals. Many gave up. The rest struggled on to the top and down into the vast Yukon Valley below.

The quickest way to reach the Klondike from here was by river. It was also the most dangerous. The clumsy open boats raced downstream through rapids and whirlpools. There was a constant threat of drowning or being smashed on the rocks.

Freezing in the ice and snow, a long line of hopeful miners make their way up the Chilkoot Pass. This was just one stage on the long, hazardous journey to the Klondike gold sites.

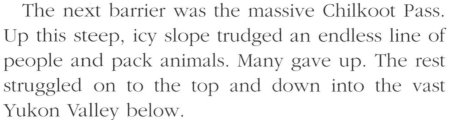

Within a few months of the Klondike Gold Rush, the population of Dawson City had grown from nothing to ten thousand people. It became known as the new capital of the Klondike.

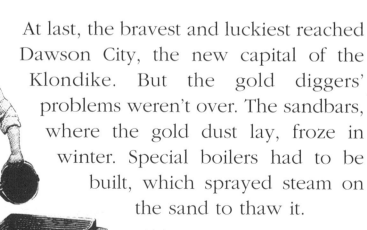

At last, the bravest and luckiest reached Dawson City, the new capital of the Klondike. But the gold diggers' problems weren't over. The sandbars, where the gold dust lay, froze in winter. Special boilers had to be built, which sprayed steam on the sand to thaw it.

A Klondike prospector with all his equipment, including a "rocker" for washing the gold.

The lost Dutchman

Dutchman Jacob Waltz was a well-known figure in the Superstition Mountains of Arizona. He would regularly ride into town during the 1870s with bags of gold to sell. But where did he get it from? No one knew. Some tried to follow him, but were later found shot dead by the trail.

Waltz hid the entrance to his mine with logs and rocks. Anyone who dared to come near it was greeted with a bullet. Eventually, Waltz himself disappeared and was never seen again. Many people have gone searching for his mysterious gold mine, but no sign of it has ever been found.

In summer, the frozen wastes turned to mud, and clouds of mosquitoes plagued the workers. The biggest danger of all came from wandering grizzly bears and polar bears, which could kill a person with a blow of their paws.

Between 1899 and 1904, over $100 million worth of gold was collected from the Klondike. After this, the boom years were over. All the easy gold had been taken, and only big mining companies could hope to make a living. The lone prospectors drifted away, leaving their derelict log cabins behind them.

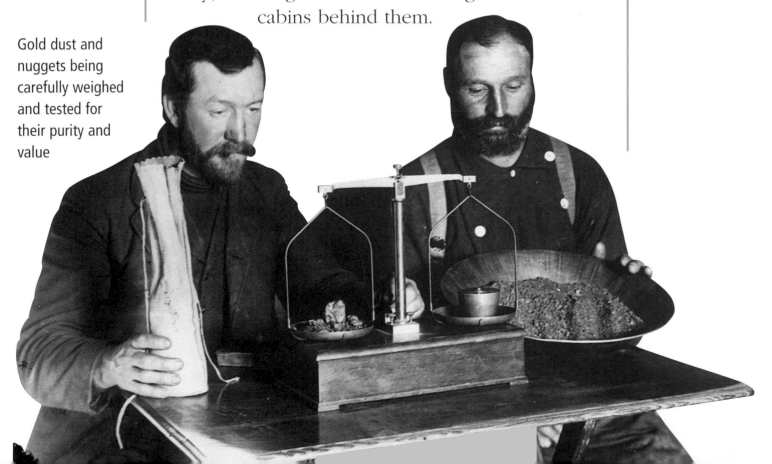

Gold dust and nuggets being carefully weighed and tested for their purity and value

JEWELS AND THEIR STORIES

For over 50 years, William van der Merwe has sifted through earth and stones searching for diamonds in South Africa. He has a claim—a piece of land 65 ft. by 100 ft.—that he works each day by hand.

THE dazzling glitter of a diamond; the wild, green glare of an emerald; the blood red glow of a ruby: These are just as beautiful and rare as gold. There's something else that can make them even more valuable: They are small and easy to hide. This means that they are easy to steal and smuggle. A precious stone can be slipped into a pocket or sewn into the lining of a coat.

A handful of such jewels can make a person rich for life. When Russia was in chaos during the revolution of 1917, many wealthy Russians fled to the safety of the West, carrying their savings in the form of precious stones. One refugee in New York sold a diamond from his hoard every year for over fifty years. Each sale gave him enough money to live on comfortably until the next year.

Precious jewels in their cut and polished states: from left to right, (top row) topaz, garnet, amethyst, emerald; (middle row) diamond, aquamarine, zircon; (bottom row) sapphire, amethyst, ruby.

The diamond that changed history

Some very special jewels have amazing stories to tell. Perhaps the most astonishing belongs to the Sancy Diamond.

This lovely stone, which was 53.75 carats, has caused murders, toppled kings, and has even started a war.

The Sancy Diamond was dug up in India in the 1500s, and then sold to Nicolas de Harley, Seigneur de Sancy, a French diplomat in Constantinople, Turkey. He in turn lent it to King Henry III of France. The king often made use of the diamond's huge value to raise much needed cash. He pawned it to a moneylender in exchange for a loan. With this, he hired an army of mercenary soldiers.

Once, de Sancy had to send the gem out of the country, in order to borrow yet more cash. It was carried in secret by a trusted servant, but he was ambushed by robbers. Without a second thought, he swallowed the diamond. The robbers were unable to find it and killed him. De Sancy ordered that the poor man's body be cut open—and there was the diamond, in his stomach!

In the early 1600s, the diamond was sold to the English Royal family. But, after King Charles I's defeat in the English Civil War (1642–48), his French wife, Henrietta Maria, fled to France, taking the diamond with her.

Below The Régent Diamond, worn by Maria Leczczynska, wife of Louis XV, King of France, at the Ball of the Clipped Yew Trees. When the Queen appeared at the ball, "her dress was covered with bunches of pearls and the two famous diamonds, the Régent and the Sancy, sparkled on her head."

Queen Henrietta Maria who took refuge in France in 1644. She was the daughter of King Henry IV of France. Her husband, King Charles I of England, was defeated by the Parliamentarians, led by Oliver Cromwell. Charles was beheaded in 1649, making him the first English monarch to be executed.

In 1789 during the French Revolution, the royal jewels were stolen and the diamond disappeared. But by 1828 it had been found, sold again, and carried off by a Russian, Prince Demidoff. A century later, the incredible adventures of the Sancy Diamond came to an end. It was bought by American millionaire William Waldorf who had it set in a tiara for his daughter.

The world's biggest hole

The Kimberley Diamond Mine in South Africa is nicknamed "The Big Hole." The first diamonds were found on the surface here in the 1860s and digging began in 1871.

Using picks and shovels, the miners hacked out more than 20 million tons of earth, creating a hole 3,600 feet deep and 1,500 feet wide. Mining ended here in 1914, but it is still the deepest opencast pit in the world.

Unused since 1914, the Kimberley Diamond Mine has now filled with water. The town of Kimberley is in the background. In its time, the mine yielded 15.5 million carats of diamonds.

Giving it a polish

When diamonds come out of the earth, they can look dull and scruffy. They have to be cut and ground to create lots of flat surfaces, or facets. Then they are polished so that they sparkle and shine.

Above Rough diamonds ready to be sorted

Above Sorting diamonds is a highly skilled job that takes six years to learn. The stones are sorted into five thousand categories of shape, size, and quality.

However, diamond is the hardest of all natural substances. It can only be cut with another diamond. Cutters use saws coated with diamond dust, and drills with diamond tips.

Above A diamond being cut with a diamond-coated bronze saw.

Left A selection of cut and polished diamonds and the various shapes that can be made. The diamonds are now checked to ensure they have been cut to the correct dimensions.

THE QUEST FOR BLACK GOLD

Striking oil at Titusville, Pennsylvania, in 1859. Drake and his men were drenched in the oil spurting from the ground.

OIL was regarded as a nuisance by the early nineteenth-century settlers in Pennsylvania. The black, sticky stuff got into their wells and polluted the water, and it seeped onto the fields, ruining crops. In the 1850s, a man in Pittsburgh began to sell the oil in bottles as a wonder medicine. Another sold it to settlers for greasing wagon wheels.

Then came a major breakthrough. In 1859 an American scientist, George Henry Bissell, discovered that a liquid fuel called kerosene could be made from oil. It was perfect for using in lamps, and kerosene soon became very popular. Suddenly, oil became a highly valuable substance and prospectors began searching for it in many parts of the continent. The trouble was that no one knew how to extract it from the ground.

"Colonel" Edwin L. Drake, who successfully struck oil in 1859. It was the start of the modern oil industry.

Striking oil

In 1859, a man known as "Colonel" Edwin L. Drake began drilling holes into the ground searching for oil for Bissell's kerosene refinery. On August 27, Drake and his men were working near Titusville, Pennsylvania, using a drill powered by an old steam engine. Suddenly, when his drill reached a depth of 75 feet, oil shot upward into the sky.

Drake's well at Titusville. Drake (center) talks to his engineer, while the laborers, who dug the well stand in the background. Oil is a fossil fuel, which is made from the heat and pressure on organic remains over millions of years.

Oil in the Ark

There is nothing new about using oil. The Bible says that Noah sealed the joints of his ark with thick, black oil called pitch. More than 2,500 years ago, pitch was used to cement the stones of the great city of Babylon.

The animals from Noah's Ark. This beautiful illustration comes from a medieval Book of Hours circa 1423.

Below Pioneer Run at Oil Creek, Pennsylvania. This photograph was taken in 1865, only six years after Drake struck oil.

He had struck "black gold." Within a few months, dozens of other oil prospectors had rushed to the area around Titusville.

The United States's oil industry grew at an incredible speed. In 1859, 2,000 barrels of oil were produced. By 1900, that figure had soared to more than 64 million barrels.

Oil is no longer used just for lighting. Now it powers cars, ships, and even power stations. Airplanes could never have been invented without oil to fuel their engines.

Today, thousands of common household items are made from oil, including carpets, detergents, toothpaste, and plastic toys. These are called petroleum products.

Treasure in the sand

In the 1920s, King Abdul Aziz was a worried man. His country, Saudi Arabia, was very poor. It had little to sell, and depended on devout Muslims for money. The Muslims made annual pilgrimage to Mecca, Saudi Arabia, Islam's holiest city. By the early 1930s, however, there were fewer pilgrims than ever. The king was more than $900,000 in debt. He was a proud man and did not want to beg.

King Abdul Aziz, who founded the powerful Saud dynasty of Saudi Arabia

Charles Crane, an American businessman, came to Aziz's aid. In 1931, Crane told Aziz that he would hire a surveyor to search for oil in Saudi Arabia. Oil had been discovered in nearby Iran and Iraq, and Crane thought it only logical that Saudi Arabia should be rich in the resource as well.

A few months later, the surveyor gave his report. Yes, he had reported, it was highly likely that oil could be found. Abdul Aziz was overjoyed. Eagerly, he signed an agreement with a United States oil company that allowed them to drill for oil. They would pay him $150,000, plus another $300,000 if they found oil.

The drillers got to work. They had little luck with their first six holes. Some produced a modest amount of oil, but the others were as dry as dust. After five years of hard work, not much oil had been found. Then, in March 1938, a seventh well was drilled over a half a mile under the surface. There it struck oil—and plenty of it. Well Number 7 began producing a steady flow of more than 2,000 barrels every day.

Immediately, the oil company paid Abdul Aziz another $600,000. This was only a tiny beginning compared with the vast wealth that was to pour into Saudi Arabia, thanks to oil. By the time

Above Well Number 7 at Ad Damman in Saudi Arabia

An oil refinery in Saudi Arabia. At a refinery, the crude oil is refined so that it can be used as a fuel, and for many other industrial purposes.

Land of flames

Baku, the capital of what is now Azerbaijan, lies on the Caspian Sea. For centuries it was a holy place for fire worshippers. The land around was lit by flames that roared and flickered from cracks in the ground. This was not the work of a fire god, however. It was caused by leaks of oil and natural gas far below the surface.

In 1860, when Azerbaijan was part of Russia, the magic left Baku forever. Oil wells were drilled and the small town quickly doubled in size. Very soon, Russia was producing nearly half of the world's oil.

Right Two oil workers in the late nineteenth century drill for oil in Baku.

Below Fire temples in Baku. They were built where flames leaped naturally from the ground.

of Abdul Aziz's death in 1953, Saudi Arabia was one of the richest countries in the world. Today, it makes over $300 million from oil every day of the year.

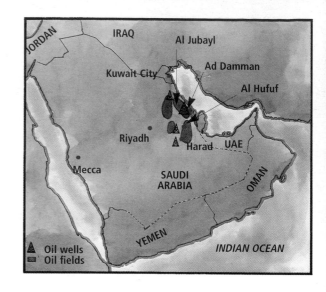

Pipeline across the ice

"Oil is where you find it—and that ain't always where you want it!" These are the words of an old-time oil prospector. The words never seemed more true than in 1968, when a huge oil field was found at Prudhoe Bay, Alaska.

But there was one big snag. Prudhoe Bay is on Alaska's northernmost coast. This means that it is inside the Arctic Circle, where the climate is very cold. For ten months of the year, the sea is locked tight with pack ice. Boats are able to reach the town only in the months of July and August. A pipeline to transport the oil was planned. It would have to cross the state from top to bottom, stretching for nearly eight hundred miles across ice that never melted.

The Endicott Oil Production Island at Prudhoe Bay in the far north of Alaska

Right An oil platform in the North Sea. Deep-sea platforms such as this have to be able to withstand harsh weather conditions. The flame burns off dangerous gases that come to the surface along with the oil.

The route of the Alaskan pipeline. The pump stations (numbered on the map) keep the oil moving through the pipe.

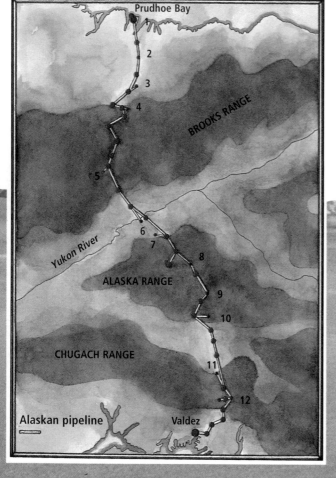

The building of this pipeline was an extraordinary feat. The pipe itself was made of steel, and had to be able to stand up to temperatures that ranged from 75°F in summer to −80°F in winter. This would cause the pipe to expand and shrink so much that it might shift as much as fifteen feet from season to season.

This problem was solved by resting the pipe on special cross beams, coated with a nonstick substance called Teflon, which allowed the pipe to slide from side to side.

Below The Alaskan pipeline crossing the Brooks Range of mountains, the first of three ranges it has to cross

There were plenty of other difficulties, too. The engineers had to make the line strong enough to withstand earthquakes. They had to build pumping stations far off in the frozen wastes, to help push the oil on its long journey. They had to take the pipeline across three mountain ranges.

Then there was the pipe itself. It was delivered in sections—97,000 of them. Each section had to be carefully welded to the next. Each welded joint had to be checked for leaks.

Protected against the biting cold, an Alaskan oilfield worker checks a pipe. Maintenance work goes on all year round.

Above An oil tanker in the calm waters of Prince William Sound at the port of Valdez, Alaska. At the end of the oil's journey through the Alaskan pipeline, it is transferred to these huge ships to be transported to other parts of the world.

Finally, there were the wild animals of Alaska to worry about. The homes and hunting grounds of wolves, wild sheep, fish, and bears had to be disturbed as little as possible. Caribou would have to cross the line on their yearly migration. To keep out of their way, engineers made a series of crossing points for the caribou by bending sections of pipe downward and burying them in the frozen earth.

The Alaskan pipeline was finally completed in 1977. Soon, 1.2 million barrels of oil were running through it every day, bringing the "black gold" from North to South Alaska.

Below After the *Exxon Valdez* oil spill in Prince William Sound, a massive cleanup operation took place.

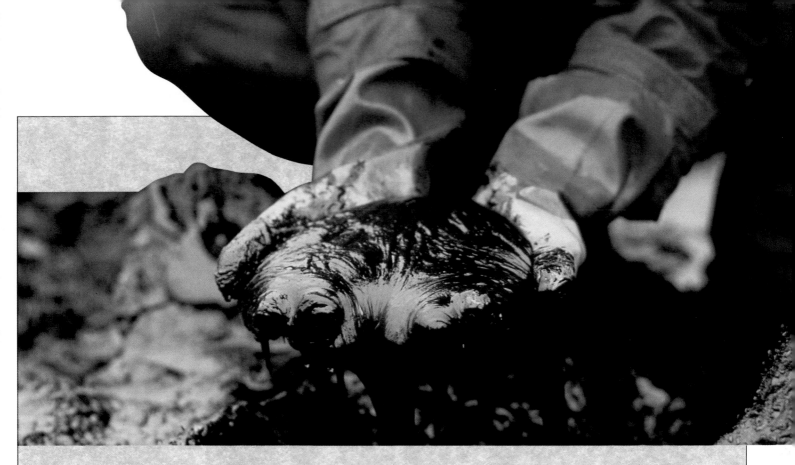

This oil sludge is what has to be cleaned up after an oil tanker spills its cargo. Not only is oil hard to remove from the coastline and sea, but it is also harmful to wildlife, whose feathers and fur become covered in it.

The Exxon Valdez *disaster*

Great care was taken to see that the Alaskan pipeline did not harm the environment. Yet even this could not prevent a tragedy. In 1989, the tanker Exxon Valdez, *filled with oil from the pipe, ran aground in Prince William Sound, on the southern coast of Alaska, and millions of gallons of oil spilled out into the sea.*

The oily water plastered itself over the long coastline, polluting beaches and harming wildlife. This environmental disaster killed over 250,000 seabirds and 1,000 rare sea otters.

DIGGING FOR BURIED TREASURE

FROM about A.D. 100 to the end of the seventh century, a people known as the Moche flourished in the desert margins of Peru, between the Andes and the Pacific Ocean. When they buried their dead, the Moche built huge pyramids of sun-baked mud as tombs, in which they placed gold, pottery, and beautiful jewelery. Because of the wealth they contained, most Moche burial sites were plundered by grave robbers, or *huaqueros,* as the Peruvians call them.

This map shows the area in Peru where the Moche people lived. The mound symbols mark where Moche burials have been found.

The rugged landscape where the Moche burial was found. The shape of the hills has been formed by rain running down the hillsides over many hundreds of years.

The sealed tomb

In February 1987, an archaeologist named Walter Alva was called to the police station in Lambayeque, Peru, to identify some artifacts stolen by grave robbers from a Moche pyramid at Sipán. The treasure that Walter Alva saw was to lead to his discovery of the finest example of an undisturbed Moche tomb ever found.

At the foot of the Sipán pyramid is a low platform, which was where the robbers had entered. They stole the artifacts they found and escaped with their treasure. But they did not know that beyond the burial chamber was a second, sealed, chamber. It was there that Alva found the body of a Moche warrior-priest.

This was what archaeologists discovered inside the undisturbed Moche burial site at Sipán.

33

Secrets in the desert

The Valley of the Kings is a lonely place, just right for hiding something. It lies below a remote cliff near the Nile River in Egypt. This was the spot chosen by Pharaoh Thutmose I, over 3,500 years ago, as a new, hidden burial ground for the

The entrance to the Valley of the Kings. It was supposed to be a secret place, but grave robbers knew about it long ago.

rulers of ancient Egypt. Earlier royal tombs had been in Pyramids, which were easy targets for tomb robbers. Thutmose had other ideas. He had his tomb dug deep into the hillside, with the entrance carefully hidden from prying eyes. Over the next five hundred years, many more Egyptian rulers were buried in the Valley of the Kings. The tombs grew larger and more complicated, some extending over 650 feet into the solid rock. Inside them were false doors and pits to trap any would-be robbers.

In spite of all these precautions, robbers found many of the tombs and stripped them of the riches they contained. Only one known tomb escaped the plunder—that of Tutankhamen, a king who had died at the age of 16. In 1922, after years of searching, a British archaeologist named

Howard Carter came upon a step cut into the rock, which led down to a door bearing the seal of Tutankhamen.

Carter described what happened: "As my eyes grew accustomed to the light, details of the room within emerged slowly from the mist, strange animals, statues, and gold— everywhere the glint of gold." The most astonishing treasure of all was the young king's coffin—or coffins. There were two outer casks of gilded wood and, inside them, a third, made of solid gold an inch thick. Inside this was the mummy itself. It was this discovery that thrilled the world.

Above Howard Carter opens a shrine door in Tutankhamen's tomb. This was the first time it had been opened for three thousand years.

Left This elaborate tent in the desert was where Howard Carter rested and examined objects brought up from the tomb in the Valley of the Kings.

The body was lavishly decorated with gold, silver, and copper ornaments and surrounded by other precious artifacts. There were other skeletons in the chamber—a servant, two women, and a soldier, who had all served the priest in life and were sacrificed after his death. There was also the skeleton of a dog—perhaps a favorite hunting dog.

Pirates and their plunder

Few people have chased treasure as savagely as pirates. They hunted down merchant ships, swarmed aboard, and grabbed whatever goods they could, slaughtering anyone who got in their way. Sometimes, their haul was a fabulous cargo of gold, silver, or coins.

Some pirate captains buried their loot on remote islands. They marked the spot with mysterious signs, or drew coded maps. However, many pirates met bloody deaths and never recovered their plunder. There are many tales of pirate treasure. In fact, very few pirate hoards have ever been found. Many of them probably never existed at all.

The storybook image of a pirate captain and his cutthroat crew, burying their hoard of treasure on a desert island

An impression of what *La Buse* may have looked like. The picture was painted by John Cruise-Wilkins, who has spent much of his life in the Seychelles searching for the treasure *La Buse* is said to have buried there.

Olivier Le Vasseur, a pirate known as *La Buse* (The Buzzard), is said to have buried the greatest hoard of treasure of all time. But where did he bury it? At today's prices, its estimated worth is about $500 million and many people have tried to find it.

Early in 1700, the British and French navies endeavored to put an end to piracy in the Caribbean. Pirates and buccaneers either fled or gave up and settled down. *La Buse* fled to the Indian Ocean where he met Captain Taylor, a notorious English pirate. *La Buse* took command of the *Victory* and Taylor the ship called *La Défense*. On April 4, 1721, the two pirates set sail for Madagascar and, en route, came across *La Vierge du Cap*, a Portuguese ship. She had dropped anchor near the harbor of St. Denis, on the island of Réunion, to undergo repairs after a violent storm. By chance, sitting in her hold was the immense fortune the pirates were looking for. With apparently little effort, immense treasure was within their grasp.

This stone is one of several on the Seychelles island of Mahe with strange markings. Many believe they were made by *La Buse* as some of the elaborate clues he left to the whereabouts of his treasure.

The mystery of Oak Island

In 1795, a teenager was exploring Oak Island, off Nova Scotia, Canada. He found a shallow pit and, hanging above it, a block and tackle for lifting heavy weights. Someone had been digging here. But who and why was unknown.

The boy and a friend began to excavate the pit. About ten feet down, they found a platform of logs. The same happened at twenty feet. Others became interested and continued to dig, finding more logs, and then a flat stone covered in strange letters. When the stone was removed, the hole filled with seawater.

For more than two hundred years, the diggers and drillers have worked at the Oak Island pit, but the mystery remains unsolved. Why was it dug in the first place, and by whom?

Two centuries of digging on Oak Island have produced no evidence about why the pit was dug.

There were "rivers of diamonds, a large quantity of gold bars, cascades of gold coins, and cases and chests of sacred church vessels and objects."

Between 1725 and 1729, it is thought that *La Buse* lived in the Seychelles with 250 of his men. There, he had plenty of time to plan a hiding place for his loot and to conceal it well. It may be hidden at Bel Ombre, a settlement on the Seychelles island of Mahe, where strange markings and signs have been found carved into the rocks. Artifacts have been found in the area that certainly date back to the time of *La Buse,* but there is no sign of the treasure itself.

Left In his cell on the island of Réunion, *La Buse* wrote this cryptogram as a clue to where his treasure lies. Whoever can decipher it may find fabulous fortune—or perhaps an elaborate hoax.

38

In 1729, *La Buse* set out for Madagascar, but a storm swept his ship onto a reef. Soon afterward, *La Buse* was captured. The French authorities condemned him to death for crimes of piracy. In his cell, *La Buse* wrote an indecipherable cryptogram that showed the location of his treasure, and how to retrieve it when it was found.

At 5 P.M. on July 7, 1730, just before his execution, *La Buse* threw the cryptogram into the air and cried out to the crowd, "Find my treasure who can." No one has, and maybe no one ever will.

Spoils of war

In April 1945, near the end of World War II, some American soldiers were on patrol in a small German town when a woman stopped them.

"I suppose you've come for the gold," she said. The woman showed them the way to a nearby salt mine. Deep inside, they came to a thick steel door. Behind it was a staggering hoard of gold bars, priceless paintings, banknotes, and other treasures.

An American soldier holding a painting by Spanish artist, Goya. This was just one of many important works of art stolen and hidden by the Nazis.

Before World War II, this American soldier was a curator of fine arts at an American museum. Here he is in Paris examining sixteenth century Italian jewelery stolen by the Nazis.

This was just a tiny part of the wealth snatched by the German armies as they had thundered across Europe, plundering churches, art galleries, castles, bank vaults, and museums. The Nazis had made sure that most of the loot was hidden.

When the war ended, the treasure had to be returned to its proper owners. A special project was begun, called Operation Rattle. Three British officers set out to find all the hidden treasure in their section of Germany.

Braddock's misfortune

The mortally wounded General Braddock is carried from the battlefield.

In 1755, General Edward Braddock was marching through Maryland to fight the French and Native Americans who threatened the English colonies. With him was a chest full of silver coins—his army's pay.

Braddock was afraid that he might lose the chest in battle, so one dark night, he crept out and buried it secretly. He meant to pick it up on the way home. The general never came back, however. He was killed by the French a few days later. The pay chest is still believed to be buried somewhere.

Within two years, Operation Rattle had unearthed thousands of wonderful objects—great paintings, priceless manuscripts, jewelery, furniture, and gold bars. The looting had not been carried out only by the Germans, however. The Soviets stole too, mainly from German museums. A great deal found its way to the Soviet Union.

In the cellar of the German castle at Kronberg, the precious crown jewels of the German royal family were hastily buried in a pit and concreted over as the allies advanced across Europe. In 1945, the castle became a club for officers. The crown jewels simply disappeared, and most have never been found again. The same thing happened to the legendary Nazi Gold Train, loaded with stolen gold, jewelery, and other valuables. The train was seized by the U.S. Army, but only a tiny portion of the gold was ever handed back.

The plan of attack by British troops under the command of General Edward Braddock, against the French at the Monongahela River in 1755

TREASURES BENEATH THE WAVES

The route of the Spanish treasure fleets from the Americas. Gold and silver from the mines inland was loaded at several ports on the mainland. Then the ships met at Havana, Cuba to sail home in force to Seville, Spain.

FINDING treasure is a difficult task. But transporting it can be even more difficult, especially when the routes of transportation involve crossing an ocean fraught with hurricanes and pirates.

These were the dangers faced by Spanish sailors four hundred years ago. In June of each year, a fleet of ships was loaded with the incredible riches taken by Spain from South and Central America. Other ships were loaded with silks, spices, and porcelain from China and Japan. When the galleons set sail for Spain, they were protected against pirates by a fleet of warships. Nothing could protect them, however, against mountainous waves and raging winds.

The silver that sank

In 1622, 28 ships set sail from Cuba. They had barely set sail on the Atlantic Ocean before they were hit by a hurricane. The fleet was tossed about by the tempest for nearly a week. Ten of the ships were lost, including three treasure galleons. One of these ships was discovered aground near the

Florida Keys. The other two had sunk with their precious cargoes of silver bars and golden coins.

It took four years for the Spanish to find one of the two wrecks, and another four years for divers to bring up most of the silver and gold inside. The third wreck, with the most valuable cargo of all, has never been located. It still lies somewhere at the bottom of the Atlantic—along with hundreds of other sunken Spanish treasure ships, scattered from the coast of Panama across to the Portuguese coast.

Bell with a bubble

To reach a shipwreck deep on the seabed, the Spanish used a diving bell. This was the first underwater vessel, and was amazingly simple. A bell-shaped metal container with an open bottom was lowered into the sea. Inside it sat one or two people. They breathed from the bubble of air trapped at the top of the bell.

The first diving suit did not appear until 1721. A British man named John Lethbridge made a barrel of wood and leather with two armholes and a glass peephole. The diver breathed the air inside the barrel.

An early type of diving bell being lowered from a boat. Hanging below the bell is a weight to help it sink. The barrel at the side provides extra air for the diver.

Disaster in pirate paradise

Port Royal, built on a remote outcrop of land on Jamaica, was once known as Sin City. For pirates, however, it was the capital of the Caribbean. During the 1670s, Port Royal harbor was full of pirate ships and its streets were full of taverns. Pirates came here to spend their ill-gotten wealth. Port Royal was a safe haven where they could sail out and attack merchant ships.

But disaster struck at midday on June 7, 1692, when a huge earthquake hit the city, burying most of its inhabitants, buildings, and ships beneath the waves. The fate of the pirate treasures became the inspiration behind many legends. It must still be there, people said, along with the rotting corpses and shattered boats and houses. So, in the autumn of 1692, the first attempt was made to find the underwater wealth of Port Royal. Some men were lowered in diving bells to the seabed. Skin divers, with no breathing equipment, followed them down.

In the sixteenth and seventeenth centuries, Port Royal, Jamaica, grew from a small fishing village into a busy port. This was largely due to the pirates who flocked there to spend their ill-gotten gains.

Modern treasure hunters examine a wreck off the Hawaiian Islands in the Pacific Ocean.

They could only recover a small part of the pirate riches, however. Work went on slowly over the next two centuries. Then, in 1907, another earthquake struck Port Royal, covering the site with fresh layers of rubble and mud. This made the task even harder. Later, searchers had to clear away the mud with suction pumps. They found hundreds of commonplace items from the old town. One lucky diver discovered a chest full of gold coins. What lies in the ruins of Sin City is still unknown.

The island of Jamaica

The Golden Man

"They stripped the prince to his skin, and anointed him with a sticky earth, on which they placed gold dust so that he was completely covered with this metal. They placed him on a raft, and at his feet they placed a great heap of gold and emeralds for him to offer to his god. When they reached the center of the lagoon, the gilded Indian made his offering, throwing out all the pile of gold into the middle of the lake."

This was the legend of El Dorado, the Golden Man. Spanish soldiers heard it as they rampaged through Peru and Colombia in search of treasure. Captured Amerindians told them that the mysterious ceremony took place on a lake called Guatavita in Colombia.

The prince is covered with mud before fine gold dust is blown all over him.

Adventurers tried for centuries to find the treasures, but all failed. Finally, in 1904, pumping equipment was hauled up the mountains, and the water was pumped out of Lake Guatavita through a tunnel. When all the water was pumped out of the lake, the workers saw that the lake floor was covered in a thick layer of slime and mud, which was impossible to walk on. Within hours, the hot sun had baked the mud as hard as concrete. This hardened mud blocked the tunnel completely, allowing Guatavita to fill up with water again.

The sacred lake is now a protected area and the gold of El Dorado—if it really exists—will probably stay hidden forever.

TIME LINE

A.D. **1850**   **1900**   **1950**

1532
●
Spaniards under Francisco Pizarro invade Peru and begin plundering Inca treasures

1692
●
Earthquake destroys Port Royal, Jamaica, burying much pirate treasure

1795
●
Mysterious pit discovered on Oak Island, Nova Scotia, Canada

1848
●
John Sutter discovers gold in California

1849–59
●
California Gold Rush

1851
●
Gold discovered near Ballarat, Australia

1859
●
"Colonel" Edwin L. Drake strikes oil at Titusville, Pennsylvania

1860
●
First oil wells drilled at Baku on coast of Caspian Sea, Russia

1896
●
George Carmack finds gold near Klondike River, Canada

1896–1904
●
Klondike Gold Rush in Canada and Alaska

1922
●
Howard Carter discovers tomb of Tutankhamen in Valley of the Kings, Egypt

1938
●
Oil found at Well Number 7 in Saudi Arabia

1977
●
Alaskan pipeline completed, stretching from Prudhoe Bay to Valdez

1987
●
Discovery of Moche warrior-priest's tomb at Sipán, Peru

1989
●
Exxon Valdez oil tanker disaster in Prince William Sound, Alaska

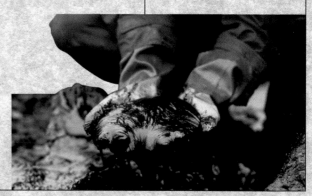

GLOSSARY

Barrel A unit of measurement for crude oil. One oil barrel holds 42 gallons.

Carat A measurement of the weight of precious stones: 1 carat = .007 oz.

Caribou A large deer that roams the Arctic regions in large herds.

Claim A piece of land staked out by a miner, prospector, or farmer, who then owns the land.

Con Artist A fraud who swindles people out of their money after seeming to be friendly to them.

Creek A small, shallow stream or inlet.

Desert To leave the armed forces without permission.

Excavate To hollow out.

Exile A person who is forced to live outside their own country.

Extract To remove something.

Facet One of the flat, polished surfaces cut on a gemstone.

Migration The movement of animals from one place to another.

Nugget A lump of natural gold.

Opencast A mine that is dug at the surface; also called a strip mine.

Pack ice Floating masses of ice on the sea, which freeze together in winter.

Pawn To leave an article with a moneylender, which is returned when the loan is repaid.

Pilgrim Someone who travels to a shrine or sacred place.

Plunder Articles that have been stolen.

Prospector Someone who looks for natural deposits of a mineral such as gold or oil.

Tiara A curved headdress made of precious metal and studded with jewels.

Wrought Metal that has been made into a specific shape by hammering or beating.

FURTHER INFORMATION

BOOKS

London, Jack. *The Call of the Wild*. New York: Puffin Books, 1983.

Pirotta, Saviour. *Pirates and Treasure*. Remarkable World. New York: Thomson Learning, 1995.

Symes, R.F. and Roger Harding. *Crystal and Gem*. New York: Alfred A. Knopf, 1991.

Van Steenwyk, Elizabeth. *California Gold Rush: West with the Forty-Niners*. New York: Franklin Watts, 1991.

FILMS AND VIDEOS

The Gold Rush (1925). Although this is one of Charlie Chaplin's finest silent comedy films, it is realistically set in the Yukon.

White Fang (1990). An adaptation of a Jack London novel, in which a young prospector in the Klondike befriends an Arctic wolf-dog.

INDEX